J A R

O F

P E N N I E S

# JAR OF PENNIES

poems by

sean karns

newamericanpress

Milwaukee, Wis. • Urbana, Ill.

newamericanpress

www.NewAmericanPress.com

© 2015 by Sean Karns

All rights reserved. No part of this publication may be reproduced, stored in a retrieval system, or transmitted, in any form or by any means, electronic, mechanical, photocopying, recording, or otherwise, without the prior written permission of the copyright holder.

Printed in the United States of America

ISBN 978-1-941561-03-4

Book design by David Bowen

For ordering information, please contact:
Ingram Book Group
One Ingram Blvd.
La Vergne, TN 37086
(800) 937-8000
orders@ingrambook.com

## TABLE OF CONTENTS

    The Son Witnesses     9

1. Jar of Pennies     13
   Home Away from the Slaughterhouse     15
   Rooms     16
   The Boy Sitting at the Piano     18
   Weeds     20
   Jar of Pennies II     22

2. The Smoke and We Rise     25
   On the Porch     27
   The Father Flag     29
   After Viewing Picasso's Guernica     32
   Angelus Novus     34

3. Fish Performance     39
   A Critical View on Love     40

|   | Outside the Bedroom | 42 |
|---|---|---|
|   | Happy Birthday | 44 |
|   | Mating | 45 |

| 4. | Cutting Down the Property Line: Father's Dream Sequence | 49 |
|---|---|---|
|   | Swing Set: A Lullaby | 52 |
|   | Fields | 54 |

| 5. | Sunday Morning | 59 |
|---|---|---|
|   | From a Tree Limb | 61 |
|   | Elbow Grease | 62 |
|   | Stories We Want Heard | 65 |
|   | My Father's Potato Death | 68 |

# ACKNOWLEDGEMENTS

Some of the poems in this volume first appeared in the following journals:

*Cold Mountain Review*: "The Boy Witnesses"

*Folio:* "Outside the Bedroom"

*Hobart:* "Stories We Want Heard," and "Happy Birthday"

*Los Angeles Review:* "Fish Performance"

*MAYDAY Magazine:* "Sunday Morning," "Cutting Down the Property Line: Father's Dream Sequence," and "Father's Potato Death"

*Pleiades:* "From a Tree Limb"

*Rattle:* "Jar of Pennies"

"From a Tree Limb" was anthologized in *New Poetry from the Midwest.*

In addition to thanking the editors at the above journals, I would also like to thank the following people: Andy Gottke, for being there from the beginning and believing in me; Russell Evatt, for your friendship and reading an earlier version of this book; Ryan Sheets, for your friendship, and for our Sunday poetry sessions, where you taught me to be a deeper reader and poet; Laura Chinchilla, for your years of support; and Okla Elliott, for your vision and friendship.

# The Son Witnesses

The son asks his father how the world works. The father looks at the car grease under his nails and cleans them with his front teeth. He pulls the globe out of the closet and selects a serrated knife, then sits. His knife feels familiar in his hand as he shows his son how to cut the globe. The son watches over his father's shoulder, wanting to know. The father hands the knife to his fellow worker. But the son is nervous, like the first time he walked around his neighborhood block alone. The son cuts the globe; it feels like cutting into a tree branch. The plastic shards fall. The father stands; his hand is on his son's back as pieces of the ocean and countries, unknown to both, fall.

1.

## Jar of Pennies

The year my mother worked
the slaughterhouse,

she came home smelling of blood:
a jar of pennies smell.

I squeezed her pant leg
and felt the dried blood

itching like wool.
She pushed me

away, not wanting any more
smells on her.

She told me about
the cows in the slaughter room,

the pigs tugging and tugging
their bodies from her grip,

and how the blood washed
from her hands. We only ate

chicken for that year.
Her ex-boyfriend knocked

on the door. The last time
he was in the house,

*

he pulled and pulled
at her arms, then pinned her

on the couch.
I sat at the dinner table,

fumbling with dinnerware.
She washed the blood

off her lips. We only needed steak
for her black eyes.

For a long year, my hands
smelled of pennies,

and my face was red with rashes
from wool. We ate chicken

and ignored the knocking
at the door. Locked it,

bolted it, made sure
we didn't make noise.

## Home Away from the Slaughterhouse

His mother works there.
She shoots a prong through cow skull
after cow skull—heads
drop and the bodies follow.

At their house, he looks out the window.
His arm is crossed with fresh stitches.
He is scared of dogs.

The summer stench of the slaughterhouse
fumes—the rot of animal parts in metal drums
wait for the incinerator.

The ash of bone is fog.
The ash of bone dries throats.
The ash of bone is piles of sand for children.
The ash of bone is a forgotten story.

He knows no other deformed town.
Everyday, statuette dogs sit
on the yard, their tongues
hang and sway.

He looks at his wound
and wants to pull
the stitch, pull it until he unravels.

# Rooms

Cows buckle when herded
into the slaughter room.

\*

A man pulls the killing trigger
in the slaughter room.

\*

Cows splash in blood
in the slaughter room.

\*

The busy drain swallows blood
in the slaughter room.

\*

Workers are ready with knives
to cut the red and white marble
carcasses in the butcher room.

\*

The conveyor belt never tires in the butcher room.

\*

Formed beef
is inspected
in the packaging room.

\*

Packed meat, plastic bags,
boxes
in the packaging room.

\*

In the loading room,
workers stack boxes of beef.

\*

In the loading room, workers
hum, soundproofing
themselves from the moaning.

# The Boy Sitting at the Piano

The broken light fixture
dangles from the ceiling,

the frameless portrait
of grandmother pinned to

the wall— ghostly. He sits
at his piano, head bowed

like prayer and plays the hallowed
piano, composing battered

music for the out-of-reach
world —the factories

rise and production halts,
crumbled silos, rusted rails.

Nature reclaims what's left.
The forgotten farmlands,

apple orchards, and Christmas
tree farm. Hand-in-hand, his

mind and fingers, merrily
he goes into them both.

If you were in the house
you'd mistaken the pinging

*

of keys as fingers tapping
the kitchen table. He makes

meaning void of meaning,
does not rethink his world,

or live by seasons:
the shifting cultivator,

the sowing of seeds,
the combine's humdrum-hum,

the inadequate salesman
behind on his quarterly

crane sales. There is no calendar
for this boy. Only ideal

emotions and ideas —
without his piano,

there's only life. Without
his art, there's only animal life.

His world is kid-delusional.
A silly boy with silly ideas.

# Weeds

> Weed *n*: is a misplaced plant that grows vigorously; one that tends to overgrow or choke out more desirable plants.

After tilling the hard
ground, I go to the garage

for packets of seeds left
from last spring. My father

forgot them on his workbench.
He showed me how to care

for the garden — dig deep
for the weeds' roots and snap

off dead leaves. My mother
left him years ago. The bench

collects junk meant to be
trashed. I poke holes with my

finger and plant tomato
seeds, then a row of peas.

I've been planting the garden
for the past four springs.

Inside the house, my mother
scrubs dishes. I don't

*

waste a nice evening after
school in the house. Her eyes

are black from lack of sleep.
She yells through the screen door —

*I work all day. The house
is a mess. What do you*

*do when I'm at work?*
I'll spend my summer in

the garden. I know what
weeds do and what her boyfriend

does. During the winter
I hid under the workbench,

blending in with junk, listening
to yells across my mother's

face. When done planting
my garden, I sit under

the shade trees and hope for
no rain, so I will have

my summer to water
and think of my father.

# Jar of Pennies II

I rub my face when I see blood. And think of my mother coming home from the slaughterhouse, the dried spots of blood on her pant leg, smelling of salt and iron. She gave me her leftover change, mostly pennies that I put in a jar. I didn't know sacrifice. Once, after dinner, I stood on top of the staircase, picking at the paint that bubbled and thumbed the gummy paint stuck under my fingernails. I waited on the staircase for my mother to come out of the bathroom. There was nobody else to cling to. I sat outside the door, ramming my palm against it, while she soaked in the bathtub. I listened to her sobs; I rattled my jar.

2.

# The Smoke and We Rise

*After viewing Walker Evan's* Bethlehem, PA

At the edge of town, a steel mill,
with smokestacks like skyscrapers, blows
smoke into the clouds—smoke that is for a moment
part of the clouds, then gone.

You never thought the smokestacks
would stop. You notice the town square
and houses that are still houses. Farther out of town,
farms still are farms, riverboats floating
on the river are still coming
and going.
There is a form to the town,
like the perfectly dug grave you stand by
in winter's mess.

There was a boy, you'll remember.
When your father left for work, you stood
at the living room window. You thought
a parade was going through town,
a procession of men walked
to work. In their hands, lunchboxes
swung like swings.

You are not that boy;
all sons leave their fathers.
You return to the ramshackle
harbor, twisted machinery
left to rust in the scrapyard, rotted
fields, the boatless river.

You are here in the cemetery,
abiding to tradition.
During the ceremony, snow-covered tombstones
fix you in their stare.

Seeing the bare oak tree,
you wonder what the cemetery
would look like in spring — the only
oak shading the small makers of
a small plot of land — enough land
to bury all who stayed. Maybe

wildflowers will grow against the fence,
blooming colorful waves around the cemetery.

You turn your shoulder from the town
slowly turning tombstone,
its histories in white ruin.

## On the Porch

*After James Agee*

The cotton absorbs
our dripping sweat.
Our backs are banged up;
us tenant farmers
are a field of umbrellas
arching over.
When the day is gone
and done with us, we
take the night
on the porch. We
wait for a breeze
to cool. We
smile some.
The porch is gray
and splintery
from years
of weather-damage.
It bows
with our weight.
The planks spring up;
the splinters can bite
your fingers
with their prickly teeth.
We don't have much
more than this porch. We
use it for more
than resting.
The porch,
sturdy or not,

is a passageway
to the otherworld.
Many of our
dead have reposed
in pine coffins
placed on the porch. We
say our peace, wait our turn
for the coffin,
and tilt our hats
to the dead.

# The Father Flag

*After viewing three paintings by Tomas Hart Benton*


**1.    "Cut the Line"**

The harbor gives birth to its machinery.
Battleships completed, bob in idleness.

Crisp flags drape over the side of a new
battleship — men swing axes and cut the line;

the battleship slides into harbor.
The crowd behind the rope barricade:

a boy straddles his father's neck, fixates
on the immaculate conceptions.

They don't understand the magnitude
of what is witnessed: gods mislead —

fathers will die, and sons, in the image
of their fathers, will follow. This is how

a nation is roused, on a harbor;
every nation was, forever and ever.


**2.    "Embarkation — Prelude to Death"**

Battleships queue the harbor. Horizons
are yellow-orange, like color formation

*

of clouds before a tornado. Formation
of soldiers carrying duffle bags.

A soldier side-glances his previous life:
His patriotic town, flag banners

stretch from brave to forgotten corners,
hung after the bombs that will be dropped,

and last supper with family; and further
back: lining toy soldiers in formation,

with father preaching "honor of serving"
and Sunday sermons on god and country.

Now the long haul to another country —
the home front will assign numbers to the dead.

3.     "Casualty"

Fire and smoke reach the sky and dictates
peace to whoever may bother to read

the signal. But don't you bother coming
to the bloody-blue waters. It's too late —

The battleships are lulled into sinking
by moans: beached dying soldiers reach

for a phantom hand. Their gesture: untouched;
their last words: unheard. Before the casualty

\*

ships launched, mothers on the confused home front
turn their ear to patriotic phrases

from their fathers. Now, bodies are strewn
across countries. Countries, with intimate

kills unwitnessed by mothers. This is
how patriotism deceives, forever and ever.

# After Viewing Picasso's Guernica

An ordinary Monday: market day
and not a stroke of work gets done.
Then a buzz above, like gods in conversation;
people are confused with their translation.
Bombs fall with patience like a stroll down
the street, a stop at a fruit stand,
selecting and sniffing for a ripe cantaloupe.

People take cover under Guernica's
sacred oak tree, where the forefathers once met.
Behind the bombardment blast, Masters
of the Universe wait and gawk at
the great Blitzkrieg experiment.
Franco's Ploughmen straddle their horned beast.
What survives will see them raring down
on Guernica's fallen oak tree, a scrapyard of limbs.

Petrified people blow out candles, crouch in shadows.
Fathers muffle their children with their hands.
Women cradle the dead in their laps;
some say spirits float out of corpse-mouths.
But that cannot be true.
If there is a heavenly light, it has turned its back.

When the waves of fire-bombings stop
and Guernica's oak tree is hauled off and burned,
it is morning. Children, shellshock-dazed and deaf,
dig bullets from rock-and-mortar walls
while unheard sparrows sing.

\*

Memories retrieved at every sight
of a jar filled with collected lead; a boy plants
a forgotten oak branch in a bomb crater
in the middle of the town square.

## Angelus Novus

*With Lines from Gerhard Scholem's
"Gruss vom Angelus"*

I am the corpse
carrying past.
The ignored messenger
riding the winds.
I am what you
want me to be—
your soothsayer;
the belief in
your belief. I
touch my feathers;
*my wing is ready
for flight.* I gaze
at the future, reluctantly.
*I'd like to turn
my back,* but the spinning
wind catches
hold of my wings
and carts me away.
Through my *timeless
travels, I've had
little luck.* All I
can do is marvel
at you. You witness,
century after
century, the fall
and rise of paradise.
I hover and wait,
wait for

a future less
traumatic. It
makes me rattle
inside, the future,
like the shifting
of rock and dirt
on the undertaker's
shovel, who buries
the past and forges
another paradise
out of tales of
muddled histories.

**3.**

## FISH PERFORMANCE

*After viewing a Lida Aboul photograph*

You place the fishbowl in the freezer. You sit on the couch and knit gloves, though it does not take long for the goldfish to freeze. The poor goldfish, when removed from the freezer, it has a permanent O shaped mouth, and the fins are held in motion. You chisel the goldfish into a novelty ice cube. You raise the goldfish to your mouth; hold it in your palm as if lifting a child's face and place a wishful kiss. A little secret kept to yourself, and I can only think of your childhood: too many goldfish flushed. Now you hold your memories in ice. I look at your lips, wanting to be your strange ritual.

# A Critical View on Love

*After reading Anthony Hecht's "Dover Bitch"*

It's so:
She did not read Sophocles, *because there is no true English translation*.
On a cliff in England, he stands
with her, wanting
to be on the French coast, thinking nonsense
of all those great French things, blah, blah, blah.
He was looking for a truer woman, but she
was an illusion by the sea.

But he is with her now. She is pretty
and alone, and like him is looking
over the Froth.
They had their moments:
A mattress on the floor and arguments
about her husband.

He is malcontent and unruly.
He flips to "The Duel" by Anton Chekhov
from a stack of books by his bed.
*I'm a cliché,* he says.
She is sprawled
in her underthings, smoking:
*We're a cliché,* she says. *We're an art house
film poster, lying here like this.*

He gets up, makes coffee.
He knows at the beginning,
every relationship

is a honeymoon.
He drinks his coffee,
looks at the chipped-paint ceiling.

Outside his window, there are great confusions.

But they are here on the cliff, not knowing
when they will end
or how one day he will think:
*How strange it is to never see again*
*the person you were with.*
He fingers her hand and she smiles.
She looks across the channel
and thinks: *The moon*
*is simply a moon, doing what it does.*

## Outside the Bedroom

1.

You slouch in the car seat
and mumble *ich will nicht ausserhalb vom Schlafzimmer.*
I believe it's about the long red light
blocks from your husband's home.

There is a pressure outside
the bedroom as potential witnesses
bike the crosswalk.

You cover your eyes
like your three-year-old daughter
scared of seeing something awful.

2.

I stand on the balcony
as you pedal away.

I want to pedal next to you
and do ordinary things—
casual walks, Café Apropos
and the Columbus museum.
But you pedal faster.

When you're gone,
I find weeks of your hair.

3.

We can go onto the balcony.
It's getting cooler. I want to show you
the large oak tree. It will hide us.

I have bread we can roll
into pebbles and toss onto the yard
to occupy the robins.

The neighbors are at work.
We have this place to ourselves.

4.

Getting used to using each other —
I watch you dress
and leave.

In the morning,
there's a pleasure
smell of you,

two sets of earrings
on the nightstand,
artifacts under dust.

## Happy Birthday

You push your bike
on the worn pathway
into the bushes.

You enter my apartment
with chocolate cake,
colorful birthday hats.

You put one on my head
and say: *I want to fuck you
while you wear your hat.*

After you leave
your husband's house,
you always have
the same expression.

We don't talk
about this.

We pretend.

We go to the bedroom
after cake. It is early
fall, and we lie in bed,
listening to the hum
of the window fan.

We don't untangle
our arms and legs.

# Mating

The finch drops
and flops around on
the sidewalk,
twitches and looks
to be dying.
The finch is a ball
of two finches
mating. They are
like us — our traumatic
tumbling in
bed, without
our sense of
separateness.
I want to be
like-intertwined
vines with someone —
to twist and hold
and eventually
rot. The finches
do their animal
wonder thing,
and I watch
the finches pull
tug and fold
together and
become
a paper crane.

**4.**

# Cutting Down the Property Line — Father's Dream Sequence

**Tire Swing**

He hacks at the thicket,
grabs hold of the blackberry
canes and bloodies his hands,

blackens them with juices.
He looks at his hands. Sees
labor: A future in

tearing down. There are children
swinging on the swinging
tire. He wants to join them.

He feels a stare. His father
sits on the porch. It's midday
and hot. The yard is dry

grass and dirt. He feels
the thorny sting to take
away what's in the house.

It keeps him hacking.
There's a silk scarf his mother
left under his pillow.

The tire swing creaks. A swing
that creaks like a deranged
mosquito singing in

\*

his ear. They swing, seeing
how far the lake is.
He rubs the dark juice

from his hands and looks at
the house, its tilted porch,
its chipped paint, the dark

tree-line; he forgets
the clink of the doorknob.


**Woods**

He goes farther
into the woods. His father stares —
faces in the bark

of every tree. He wants
to drop a match on the everywhere
leaves. He hears the twisting

of the door knob. He hides
his face with the scarf from
the footsteps and the black

polished boots under the bed.
He gathers the sturdiest
tree limbs he can pull

with his thirteen years of strength.
With his hatchet he cuts
the limbs into logs,

\*

hammers them around a tree.
He stole rope from
his father's workshed.


**Fortress**

He peeks out of the hollow
of the oak tree. He slips
on the dewy ground.

His father's dream-weight pushes
down on him. He swipes mud
from his lips. The insects

sound like the twisting
of the doorknob. So do the branches
falling, the crunch of leaves

under his feet, and the rustle
of the treetops' leaves. He throws
the rope over a tree limb,

dollies up his scarf, hatchet
and hammer. There's no
higher place for him
to throw his rope.

## Swing Set: a Lullaby

On the swinging swing
you become a bird
and fly your pattern —
back and forth.

Your legs are wings,
the house is a broken nest —
no one sings
lullabies. When you
lift from the ground,
the house lifts with you.
When you touch the ground
the house touches down.

Everything swings with you.
The night swings in.
The half-moon
is a crooked thing swinging.

You want to swing
in your mother's arms —
she is not home.

She swings a butcher knife
in the slaughterhouse.

You want to swing
from your father's arms —

*

he is swallowing
swinging swigs
from the bottle.

In your bed, you hear
the swings swinging —
*creak, creak, creak.* It is the song
you fall asleep to.

## Fields

At the end of summer
the Midwest cornfields
were death-yellow.

The cornstalks in the heat-breeze
fluttered their death-rattle.

*

My childhood home
was tucked between
death-yellows.

*

When the combine hummed
its night-song,

the death-yellow's leaves
waved goodbye.

*

In the morning, the death-yellows
now stubble fields
became ankle-splinters.

\*

I stood at the edge of the property-line.
Glaring at the low-lying hills
lost between here and there
wanting, simply, to have

an unknown source
lift me to a new, unnamed
geographical terror.

5.

## Sunday Morning

After his first heart attack,
I play with a bullet,
thumb the buffed casing
and pick at the lead.
A week's worth of beer cans,
pop cans, and burnt-out
light-bulbs clatter in
the back seat with the .22
and 9mm.
The truck rattles down
the gravel road, and we
stop by our Sunday field.
The target's backdrop is
made of railroad ties stacked
five high. I place the cans
and light-bulbs in a processional
line. He glares down and says,
"I'm going to show you
how to use these pistols."
I'm eight. I drop the gun
in the mud and quickly
pick it up, use my shirt
to clean it, but he jerks
the gun from my shaky
hand. He stands behind me
with his arm reaching out,
his hand grips around mine
as we both stare down
the barrel. His finger
pulls my finger against

the trigger. What keeps us
whole is ammunition.
He is the cold casing.
I want to be the hot
lead that splits from
the chamber.

## From a Tree Limb

Outside my house, a gutted buck dangles
from a tree limb.  Two men pull the buck's hide
like tugging on a bell rope in a tower.
Their children swing on the swing set.
I've never seen a deer slaughtered,
never seen many things slaughtered.

I once saw my father gut a squirrel.
*Doesn't smell right*, he said.  He put the squirrel
an inch away from my face.
*Sniff it*, he said. I smelled it, sucked in the odor
like my last breath and shrugged my shoulders
not knowing what I was sniffing for.
He dug a hole in the yard.
*You got to dig the hole deep enough,*
he said. *So the dogs can't smell it and dig it up.*

I wonder where the heart is,
where the spleen is,
if the men will leave the buck
disemboweled in two locations.

I press my face to the screen door.
A child pets the hide splayed over
the laundry line, the other watches
the hacking off of hooves.

## Elbow Grease

When Dad was booted from the paper
mill, and with no foreseeable work,
he went about the house and fixed

the dripping faucets, tightened the floor planks,
and painted the home Mom's favorite
baby blue. He did enough to deem

himself worthy of the role *man
of the house*, though, he took to drink
often enough for Mom to reconsider

that thought. When the house quieted
at night, he sat on the porch swing,
with fireflies flickering and

the moon doing its moon thing.
When he thought he was alone,
he dropped his guard; cried a little

and cursed the world. With his finger
in the lip of the rotgut whiskey
bottle, he swayed the rotgut gingerly

over the arm of the swing, and contemplated
the way of the world and all
rejected things. "This ain't a good

example for your boy," Mom sternly
said, one evening. He took a long
swig and looked at me spinning

\*

on the tire swing, getting dizzy
in the evening. My spring jacket
ballooned from the breeze. "Time to show

you about elbow grease," he hollered.
I overheard that phrase from Dad's
friends when they fiddled around

in the garage and drank on weekends —
"Put some elbow grease behind it,"
or "It takes some elbow grease,"

they'd say. A little elbow grease,
I learned: the burden of muscle
and providing, the burden of

failed big dreams. It was a pride thing:
work. Dad's grease burned out. That's manhood.
We stood by the garden one morning.

Last year's garden was spiny.
"Today's the last frost. The best day
to plant," he muttered, and lifted

the hoe behind his shoulder, swung
and cut the hard ground, swung again
and again till he had a row

of turned up dirt. He straddled the row
and kneeled and crumbled the chunks.
He pulled the dirt into a long

mound. His sweat smelled of rotgut.
"Do like I did." He shoved the hoe
into my chest. I went down a

*

length of land, chopping. "Feel that?" he slurred. "Naw," and swung. "That's work," he said. Digging at someone else's dirt."

## Stories We Want Heard

My dad had a scar on his shoulder —
an inch of puffy flesh that shined
like a pink marble. I was a boy

when I first saw it. He took off
his tee-shirt after mowing the lawn
and wiped the sweat from his face.

He sat on the front porch. I tried
to pop it. I thought it was a boil.
It was too hard to dig my finger into.

*I was stabbed in Nam.* He brushed
my hand from his shoulder. *I was
the last man standing in my platoon.*

*Then, out of nowhere, I was
surrounded by Gooks. I fought them
off but not before one stabbed me.*

*But I got him too. Then I waited for
rescue. I spent a day and a night
hiding.* I imagined him, a newly

minted war hero, hiding.
His forehead and eyes bobbing up
and down in a dirty river

like a crocodile as he waited
to make his move to safety.
During recess, I told the story

*

to my classmates. In my version
he saved his entire platoon.
*Your dads couldn't have done it,* I said.

A punch was thrown by Jimmy.
I dropped like a dead Gook. *My dad's
a hero,* Jimmy said, and kicked me.

I stomach-crawled behind an oak tree,
held my jaw with my hand, looked around
the big oak that dwarfed me. I scoped

the playground for a passage
to the school entrance. In math class,
I thought of the story I would tell

my dad. How I rolled across the dirty
and rocky playground, my fists
swinging at the class bully.

That I'm a heroic soldier like him.
At home, with my swollen eye
and dirty clothes, I said, *he tried*

*to take my lunch money. Everyday
he tried.* He put his hands together
and massaged his palm with his thumb.

His callused hands were un-sanded
lumber across my arm or shoulder
when he touched me fatherly for

encouragement, something good I'd done.
I was slouched on the couch. *Sit up straight,*
he chimed in, breaking my trance.

\*

I pushed myself up with my hands.
*Go to your room*, he said. I slumped
my shoulders, dragged my tail to my

room. *There is always punishment,*
he said, and grounded me from
going outside for a week.

Each night he came in and took his
index finger across the dusty
surfaces of my bedroom and handed

me a bottle of Pledge and an old sock
to clean with. As a teenager,
I went camping with my uncles.

They told stories about their father.
They laughed when I told the story
of my dad's scar. *Nam? He was stationed*

*in Berlin.* A bar fight, they said.
He picked a fight with a larger,
drunker man. *Just picked your dad up*

*like a bag of trash and threw him through*
*a table. A broken pint glass gashed*
*his shoulder.* I touched the inch scar

on my arm—a dog bite from when
I was eight. I thought of stories I'd tell.

# My Father's Potato Death

*After viewing Anke Merzbach's* Bedrohlich

The Irish weather demands a green umbrella
but I prefer green over black.
I see green in ways
the morning light comes up over
the green trees that separates
the city from the green-plastic covered
potato mounds.

Being a crop inspector is serious business.
There's been a few cropped
heads because of men
with hatchets who remember
the potato scare. My father
was on duty protecting the crops,
and I found him headless holding
an umbrella.        His death reminds
me of the economics of a potato:
potato vodka for Russians
or competing with them Idahoans;
those fancy red rich people potatoes.
All fortified by hatchet men.

I took up the post in honor
of my father, and I will bleed
out the men who steal my potatoes
and use their blood to fertilize crops.
I will tuck them in a makeshift plastic
greenhouse and plant their heads,
calling them head mounds.

\*

I eat fried potatoes in memoriam
of the headless.  I fire a twenty-one
potato gun salute into the green
haze released from the potato factory.

**SEAN KARNS'** poetry has appeared in *Pleiades, Rattle, Los Angeles Review, Folio, Cold Mountain Review, MAYDAY Magazine,* and elsewhere.

www.ingramcontent.com/pod-product-compliance
Lightning Source LLC
LaVergne TN
LVHW041346080426
835512LV00006B/631